W9-BNS-846

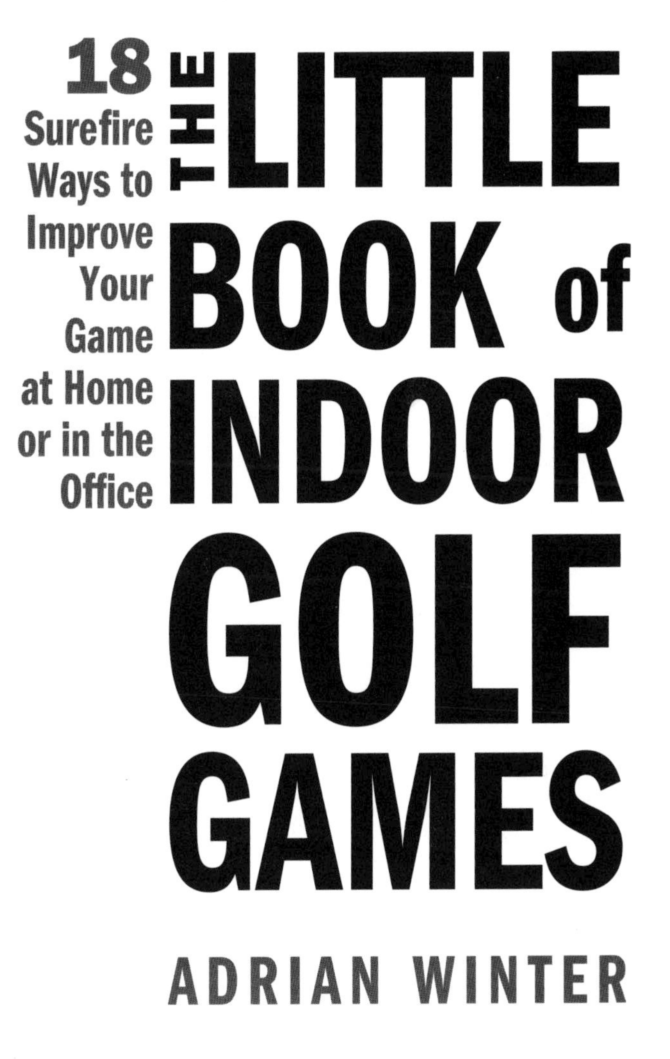

18
Surefire
Ways to
Improve
Your
Game
at Home
or in the
Office
THE
LITTLE
BOOK of
INDOOR
GOLF
GAMES
ADRIAN WINTER

sourcebooks

Cover design by Cyanotype Book Architects
Cover image © janmleung/iStockphoto.com

This publication is designed to provide accurate and authoritative information in regard to the subject matter covered. It is sold with the understanding that the publisher is not engaged in rendering legal, accounting, or other professional service. If legal advice or other expert assistance is required, the services of a competent professional person should be sought.—*From a Declaration of Principles Jointly Adopted by a Committee of the American Bar Association and a Committee of Publishers and Associations*

Published by Sourcebooks, Inc.
P.O. Box 4410, Naperville, Illinois 60567-4410
(630) 961-3900
Fax: (630) 961-2168
www.sourcebooks.com

Library of Congress Cataloging-in-Publication Data is on file with the publisher.

Printed and bound in the United States of America.
SB 10 9 8 7 6 5 4 3 2 1

CONTENTS

FOREWORD

I started playing golf when I turned six years old. My dad took an old putter down from our loft and gave it to me for my birthday along with a set of old balls. I remember vividly the excitement of unwrapping the present and the realization that I had my very own golf club.

Around that time we paid regular visits to my grandparents' house for family gatherings, and in an attempt to keep me amused, the putter was often packed in the car. At one such get-together, I remember my aunt enticing me into the hallway with a $1 bill. She laid it down on the carpet and told me I could keep it if I was able to putt a ball from one end of the hall to the other and make it come to rest on the bill. Feeling safe in the knowledge that not only would I be kept quiet for hours but also that her money was safe, she left me to it.

I remember trying over and over again. Gradually I got used to the weight of the putt and my line became more consistent, but even when both looked to be perfect, the ball would either finish just short or trickle tantalizingly past the money. Time and time again I would get agonizingly close only to watch as the ball missed landing on the bill by a fraction.

By this point, I remember, various members of my family had come to the hallway to see how I was faring. While they stood watching me as I continued to try to claim my prize, it finally happened. I sent the ball rolling toward the target, and just as it looked to be stopping short, it caught the front of the bill and found just enough momentum to trickle on. I'd done it…and with everyone watching!

I look back on that day as the moment my love of golf started, and even now, nearly thirty years later, it hasn't diminished. I still regularly practice my putting with games I have invented (many of which appear in this book), and I consider putting to be the strongest part of my golf game. I hope you not only have a lot of fun with this book, but soon consider putting the strongest part of your game as well.

—Adrian Winter

INTRODUCTION

"I don't fear death, but I sure don't like those three-footers for par."
—Chi Chi Rodriguez

"I enjoy the oohs and aahs from the gallery when I hit my drives. But I'm getting pretty tired of the awws and uhhs when I miss the putt."
—John Daly

Putts are the most common shot in golf. They make up around 40 percent of all strokes in a round, so it's no surprise that improving your putting is one of the biggest keys to lowering your golf score. While it may not be possible to sink every putt every time—even professional golfers miss around half their putts from 6 feet away—the good news is there is an easy way for all of us to improve. That way, quite simply, is to practice, and this book will help you do just that.

The Little Book of Indoor Golf Games contains 18 "holes" of fun and increasingly challenging games that are specifically designed to improve your putting in the comfort of your home or office. In contrast to the traditional methods of repetitive drills or hitting into a ball-returning machine, this book introduces different and exciting ways to practice through games. Whether you're a single-figure handicapper or picking up a putter for the first time, playing and practicing the games in this book will improve your putting in a fun but purposeful way.

The games are designed to develop the two key elements of putting; **line** (direction) and **length** (speed). To improve the line of your putts, targets in the games are often set at a gap of 4 ¼ inches—the diameter of a golf hole. Sometimes, to sharpen your accuracy, you are required to aim at just one single tee. To work on your length, some games require you to place a line of string (which you must avoid putting over) 2 feet behind the target area. This helps you develop the important habit of putting at a speed that would take the ball beyond the hole but stop soon after it. It's very important not to putt too far past the hole because, as research by putting guru Dave Pelz shows, professional golfers rarely miss a putt from 2 feet but miss up to 15 percent of those tricky 3-footers. Pelz also says that an ideal putt should have enough speed to finish 17 inches past the hole. This gives the ball the best chance to hold its line and still drop into the hole.

The section in the book called "12 Simple Steps to Becoming a Better Putter" can be used to develop a sound technique and help you address any bad habits. As your skill improves, refer to the sections called "Want a Challenge?" that offer tips on how to steadily increase the level of difficulty of each game. In addition, all suggested measurements in the book are flexible so you can gradually vary them to make each game a suitable test of your own ability.

The 18 games are suitable for all ages and require little more than basic golfing equipment—a putter, balls, and some tees. You don't need a large area in your home to play since each game can be adapted to fit whatever size space you have. Although designed for playing indoors on a carpet, there is no reason why the games can't be played outside too, perhaps in a backyard or on a practice putting green.

This book is designed for one, two, or more players making it suitable for you to play either on your own or with family and friends. If you're interested in a bit of friendly competition, play the Indoor Open Championship—a round of all 18 holes—and see who the overall champion is. A section at the back of this book explains how to play and keep score.

I wish you many hours of enjoyment as you play your way through the games. By practicing your putting indoors, you'll soon see the results outside on the golf course. Finally, remember to keep track of your progress and always keep aiming to improve. As golf legend Ben Sayers once said, "A good player who is a great putter is a match for any golfer. A great hitter who cannot putt is a match for no one."

12 SIMPLE STEPS TO BECOMING A BETTER PUTTER

There is no one correct way to putt, and even the professionals have different putting styles and techniques. However, having a firm grasp on these basics will go a long way toward helping you improve your putting.

Line it up and imagine the putt–Before you play the shot, try standing behind the ball, keeping it in line with the hole. Study the path you want the ball to take, and picture exactly how you want the putt to go.

Stand correctly–Place your feet about shoulder-width apart, and position the back of the ball in the center of your stance. Don't stand with your weight on your heels—it should be slightly biased toward your toes.

Line up your feet–Imagine a line from one big toe to the other and make sure it's pointing exactly parallel to the direction you want the ball to go.

Position your eyes directly over the top of the ball–This is important for helping you see the line of the putt more clearly.

Line up the putter–Place the center of your putter head directly behind the ball, and line it up carefully. Some putters have a line on them that you can use to help you aim.

Relax–Relax your whole body, especially your arms, and bend your knees and elbows slightly. Whatever your style of grip (there are several different grip types; you can research to find the best option for you), it's also important not to hold the putter too tightly. Imagine you're holding a full tube of toothpaste with the lid off and you don't want any to come out.

Keep your head still–Try not to move your head at all while you are putting. This will help to keep the rest of your body still, making your stroke more consistent.

 **Swing straight**–Swing the club evenly, like a pendulum, both back and forth in a straight line. This line should be the direction you want the ball to go. The putter head should still be in line with the hole when you finish your swing.

 **Keep your wrists locked**–Don't rotate your wrists during the backswing or follow-through. Stay relaxed, but keep them locked in position. Similarly, be careful not to twist your forearms during the stroke.

 **Hit "through" the ball**–It is important to hit through the ball and not at it. In other words, always follow through after you've made contact with the ball, keeping a smooth stroke at all times. The backswing and follow-through should be equal in length.

 **Be confident**–Confidence is a big part of successful putting, so believe in your ability to make the shot!

 And finally…**PRACTICE, PRACTICE, PRACTICE**!–The more you practice, the better you'll get, so enjoy this book and keep trying to improve.

CLOCK GOLF

A simple game to help with those tricky short putts. Can you putt around the clock and hit all twelve targets in a row?

ONE PLAYER:

1. Place an upturned tee in the center of the room. Position twelve more tees in a circle, each about 3 feet away from the center tee.
2. Putting from the center tee, try to knock over the tee positioned at one o'clock.
3. Continue putting around the clock, starting each time from the center, taking one attempt at each tee.
4. After all twelve attempts, count how many tees you successfully knocked over. Keep putting until you are able to hit all twelve tees in a row.

TWO OR MORE PLAYERS:

1. Follow the instructions above with each player taking a turn to make twelve attempts on his/her own clock.
2. The player who knocks over the most tees is the winner. If it's a tie, the game goes to sudden death, with players now putting on the same clock. Each player takes a turn to hit the one o'clock tee. If a player misses, he/she is out of the game. All successful players move on to the two o'clock tee. The last player left is the winner.

Want a challenge?

- Try moving the tees farther away from the center. Can you still knock over all twelve?
- Position the twelve tees at different distances from the center, forcing you to vary the length of each putt accordingly.

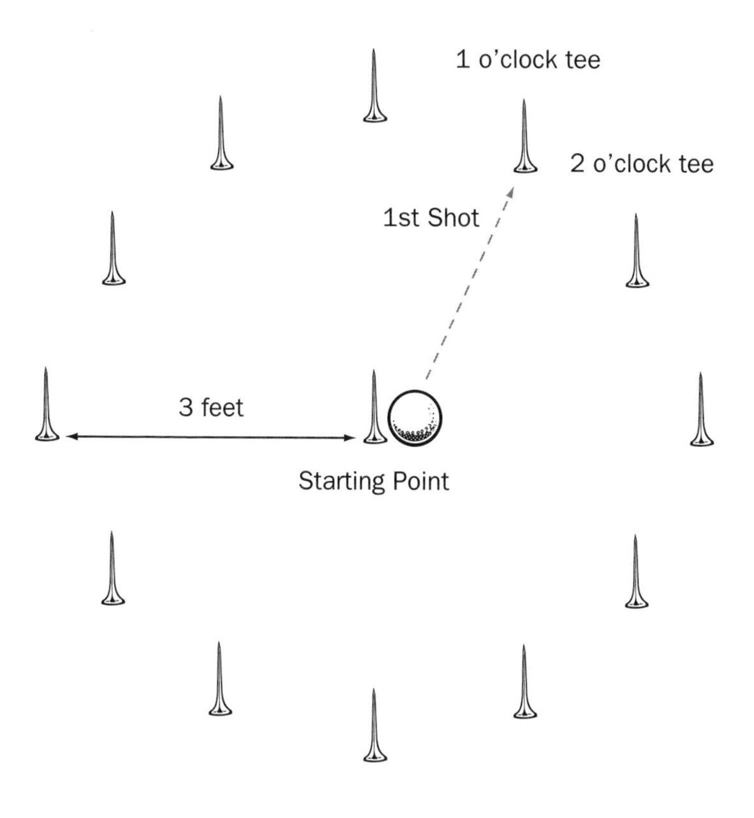

EVERY PUTT COUNTS

A fun game to help improve both line and length. Hold your nerve to score as many points as you can.

ONE PLAYER:

1. Line up five tees at the intervals shown, and place a length of string 2 feet behind the tees. The gaps between the tees make up four scoring segments—the smallest gap is the exact diameter of a golf hole.
2. Stand 4 feet away and putt eight balls, aiming to get each ball through one of the gaps. Award yourself points according to which gap a ball goes through. Be careful—if a ball crosses the string, no points are awarded for that putt. If you knock over a tee, your total score goes back to zero.
3. The aim is to accumulate at least 20 points from your putts. If you are successful, move back 1 foot and try again. How far from the tees can you go?

TWO OR MORE PLAYERS:

1. Following instructions 1 and 2 above, players should take turns to putt their balls and accumulate points.
2. The winner is the player with the highest total score. If it's a tie, take one more putt each until a winner is determined.

Want a challenge?

- Make the gaps between the tees narrower, or remove the one-point segment altogether.

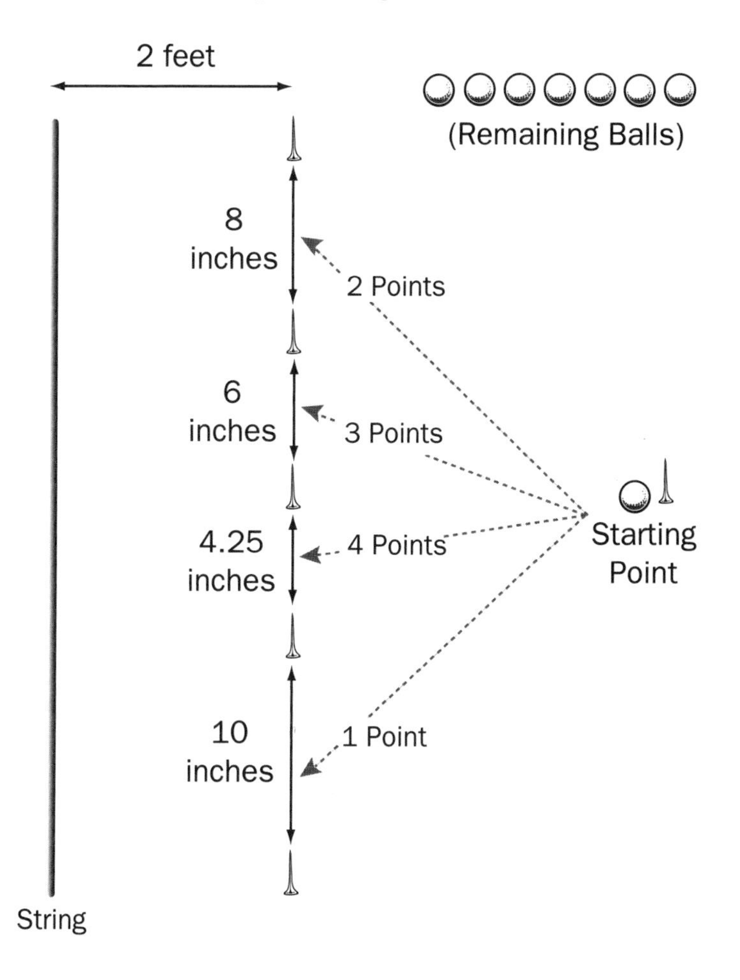

SLALOM GOLF

A challenging game to help improve your touch. Try to putt a slalom route around the tees without straying off course.

ONE PLAYER:

1. Take seven tees and place them in two staggered lines at the distances shown.
2. From the starting point, putt a ball around Tee 1, leaving a clear path to Tee 2. Continue putting around the course, trying to steer a path around each tee in turn. Finish by knocking over the target tee.
3. The challenge is to finish the course in just six strokes. If you knock down any of the first five tees or stray off course, you must start over.

TWO OR MORE PLAYERS:

1. Follow instructions 1 and 2 above, and have each player take a turn tackling the course. If a tee is knocked over (excluding the target tee), the offender can continue to the next tee but with two penalty strokes added to his/her score.
2. The player who completes the course in the fewest number of shots is the winner. If it's a tie, settle the game by starting at Tee 1 and trying to knock over the target tee in one putt. If all players miss, the ball that finishes closest to the target tee is the winner.

Want a challenge?

- Place the two lines of tees wider apart or the tees in each line closer together.
- Add more tees to make the lines longer.
- Move the target tee farther away.

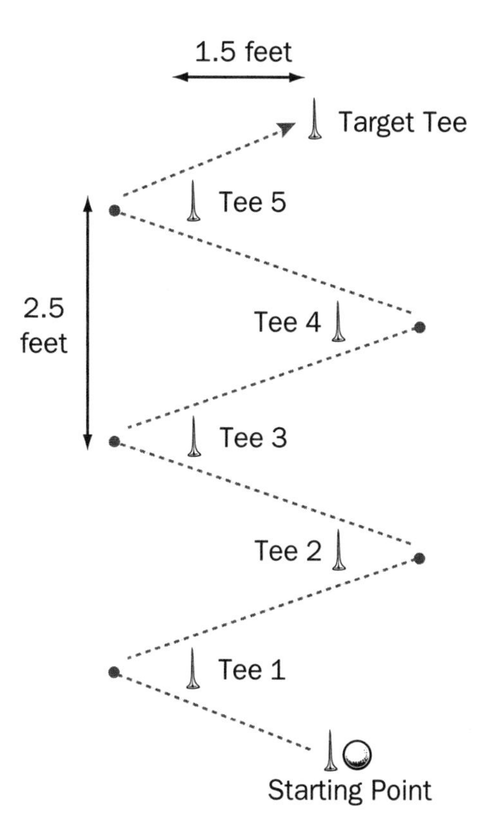

4 THE FIVE-BOX CHALLENGE

A game of skill to improve the weight of your putts. Can you putt just one ball into each box?

ONE PLAYER:

1. Create five boxes by arranging twelve tees at the intervals shown in the diagram.
2. Starting about 4 feet away, take five balls and try to putt the first ball into Box 1.
3. If successful, do not remove the first ball, and try to putt the second ball into Box 2. Accuracy is very important here, as you'll need to avoid hitting the first ball or blocking your path to the other boxes.
4. Now try to get the third ball into Box 3 and so on. The aim is to putt just one ball into each box in order, without removing any of the previous balls.
5. If two of your balls finish in the same box, a ball rolls outside the area of the boxes, or you knock over a tee, you must start over.

TWO OR MORE PLAYERS:

1. Set up and play the game as outlined above. Player 1 goes first and sees how many boxes he/she can occupy with the five balls. Player 1's balls are then removed, and the next player takes his/her turn. The player who occupies the most boxes is the winner.
2. If the game ends in a tie, players should take turns putting into Box 5. The last player to miss wins.

Want a challenge?

- Change the dimensions of the boxes to make them shorter or narrower.
- Add more boxes and putt more balls.
- Gradually move back and start from farther away.

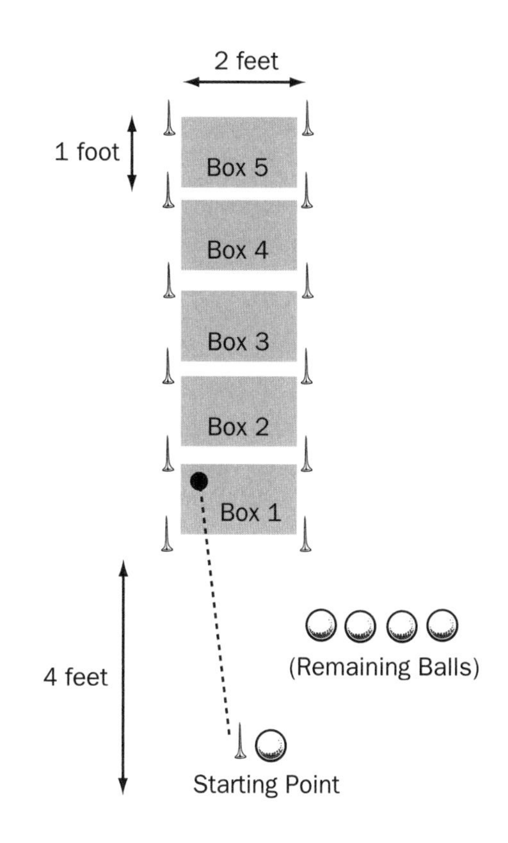

TEN-PIN GOLF

A simple test of accuracy. You'll need perfect aim and a bit of luck to get a strike!

ONE PLAYER:

1. Arrange ten tees in a triangle formation with each tee positioned approximately 1 inch apart. Place a length of string 2 feet behind the tees.
2. Starting 3 feet away, try to knock over all the tees in just two putts, without either ball crossing the string.
3. If successful, keep moving back 1 foot at a time and try again.

TWO OR MORE PLAYERS:

1. Set up the game as described above, and agree on a starting point a suitable distance away.
2. Players take turns to putt a maximum of two balls and aim to knock down as many tees as possible.
3. One point is awarded for each tee knocked over. If *either* ball crosses the string, the player's turn is over and no points are awarded for either putt. If the player is able to successfully knock down *all* the tees with the first putt (a strike), there is no need to play the second ball and he/she is awarded twenty points for that turn.
4. Keep score until each player has had five turns. The player with the highest total score is the winner. If it's a tie, take one more putt each. The player who knocks over the most tees is the winner.

Want a challenge?

- Place the tees wider apart or use more tees to make a bigger triangle. You may need to play with three balls.

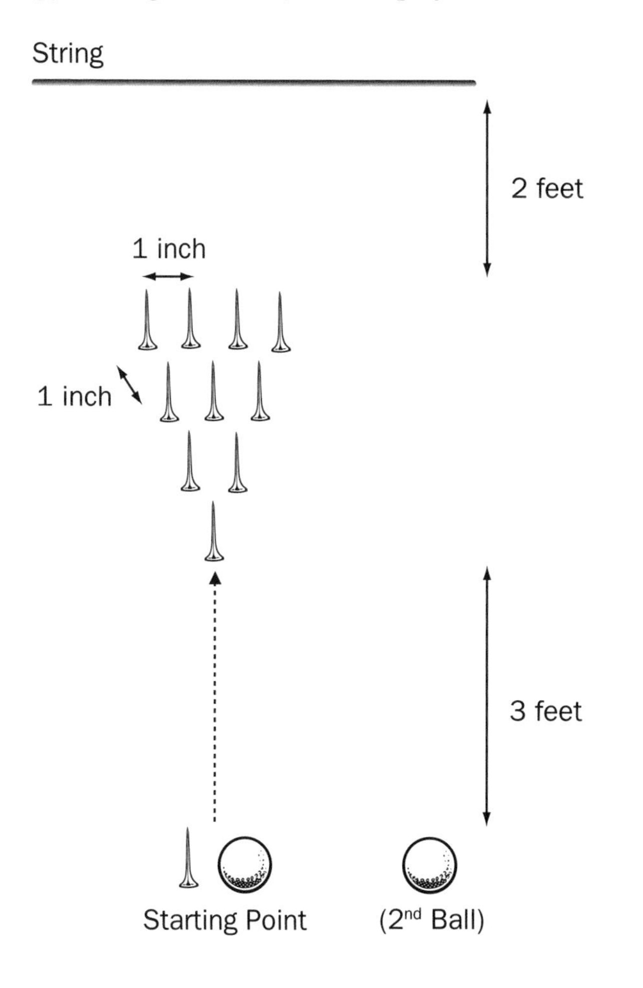

LAST BALL STANDING

An exciting game to practice both line and length for two or more players. Who will have the last ball standing?

TWO OR MORE PLAYERS:

1. Place a target tee on the floor, and agree on a starting point a suitable distance away. For the first round of putts, each player has four balls and putts alternately, aiming at the target tee. (If possible, use a different color or brand for each set of balls.)
2. The aim is to get all your balls as close to the target tee as possible without knocking it over. The ball that is *farthest away* from the tee after all the balls have been played is removed from the game.
3. However, if the tee is knocked down, the round is instantly over, and the player who causes it to fall on his/her turn loses a ball.
4. The second round then begins with a player now having only three balls to putt. The loser of the previous round should putt first.
5. The game continues until all but one player runs out of balls. The player with the last ball(s) standing is the winner.

Want a challenge?

- If a player causes an *opponent's ball* to knock over the tee, the opponent's ball is removed from the game.

- Introduce a handicap system where the person with the last ball standing from the first game starts with only three balls in the next game.

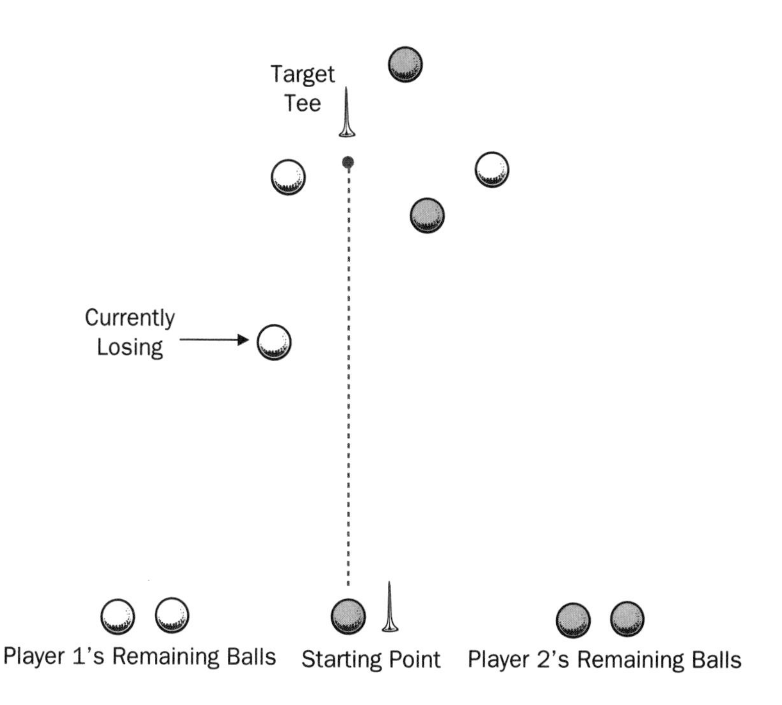

MINEFIELD

Putt through the minefield in as few strokes as you can. Placement is key here.

ONE PLAYER:

1. Put a tee at each corner of a 3 x 3 foot square, and place sixteen more tees at random within the square. Position a length of string 2 feet from the far side of the square.
2. Line up five balls about 2 feet away. Try to putt each ball through the minefield in a maximum of two putts, without knocking over any tees or crossing the string.
3. If you are successful, move back 6 inches and try again.

TWO OR MORE PLAYERS:

1. Follow the instructions above with each player taking a turn to putt all of his/her five balls.
2. If a ball successfully passes through the minefield in one stroke, award two points for that putt. If two strokes are needed, award one point. If three or more strokes are taken, a tee is knocked over, or the ball crosses the string, no points are awarded for that putt.
3. For an added challenge, players can create the minefield for their opponents and subtract a point if a tee is knocked over. Score the most points and win.
4. If the game ends in a tie, move back to about 6 feet away. The first player to successfully putt through the minefield in one shot is the winner.

Want a challenge?

- Alter the shape of the minefield to make it longer and narrower or try placing more tees inside.

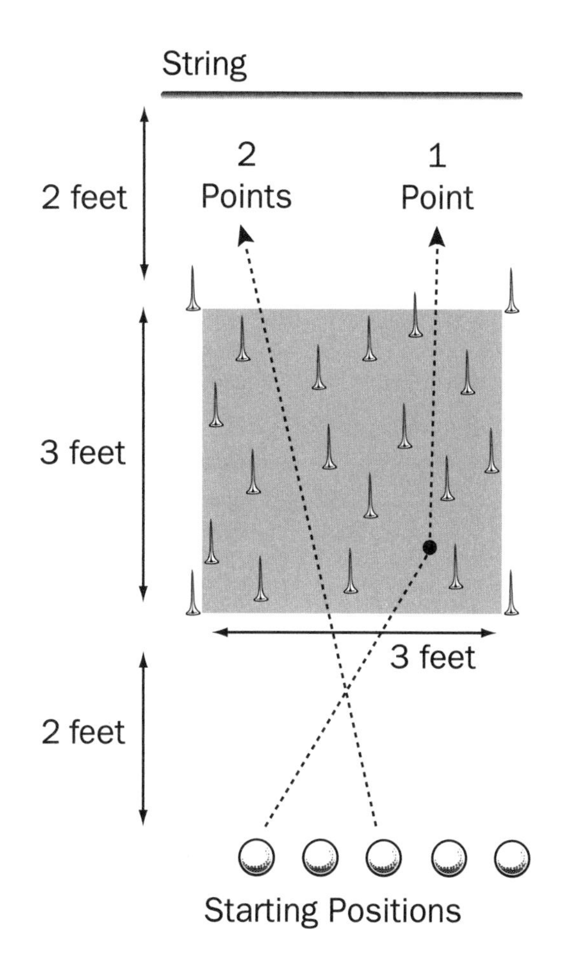

DISTANCE CHALLENGE

A simple game to help with different-length putts. How far from the target can you go without missing twice?

ONE PLAYER:

1. Place two tees 4¼ inches apart (the diameter of a golf hole) at one end of the room with a length of string 2 feet behind them.
2. Starting 2 feet away, try to putt five balls in a row between the tees. If a ball crosses the string, misses the gap, or knocks over a tee, it is unsuccessful.
3. If all five putts are successful, move back 1 foot and try again. If you miss only one putt, play all five balls again from the same distance. If you miss with two or more balls, you must return to the original starting point and begin the game again.
4. The challenge is to see how far from the tees you can get.

TWO OR MORE PLAYERS:

1. Follow instructions 1 and 2 above. The player(s) with the highest number of successful putts gets a point.
2. The winner chooses a new starting point, and all players try again.
3. The winner of each round wins a point and chooses the next starting position (closer or farther away). The first player to accumulate five points is the overall winner.

Want a challenge?

- To practice the optimum putting speed, aim to make each putt finish 17 inches past the tees.
- Make the target just a single tee and try to knock it over.

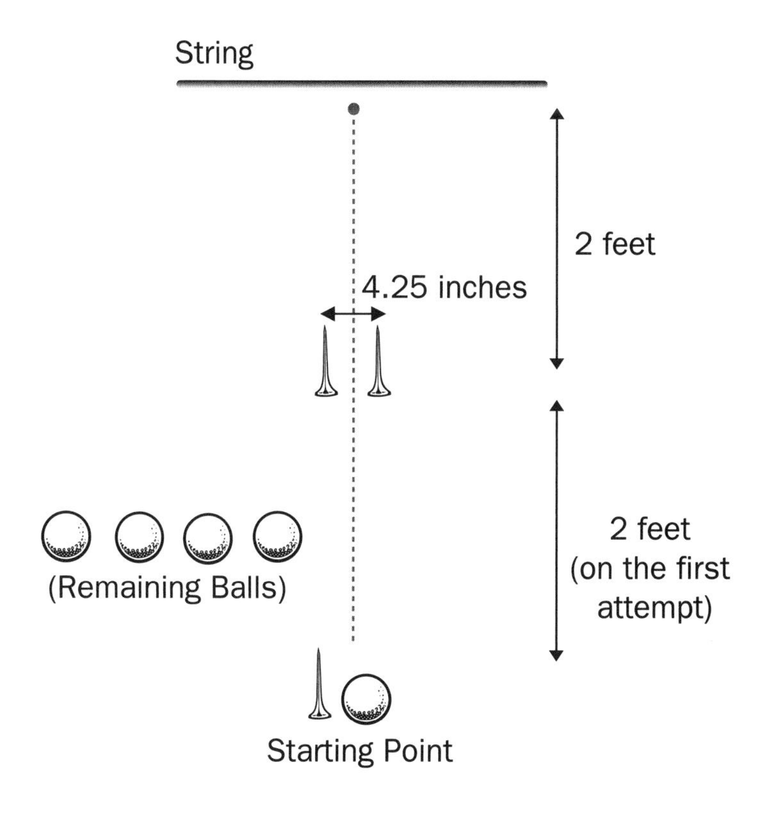

TARGET PRACTICE

A fun game that requires pinpoint aim. Can you achieve the maximum score of seventy points?

ONE PLAYER:

1. Take a complete set of one suit from a deck of cards. Arrange them on the floor in two rows, placing the cards in the order shown.
2. Place one tee in the middle of each card and a length of string 2 feet behind the back row.
3. Starting about 6 feet away, putt eight balls in a row and try to knock over a tee with each ball. Each tee is worth the same number of points as the card it is sitting on. The Ace is worth one point, and the Jack, Queen, and King are each worth ten points. If a ball crosses the string, no points are awarded for that shot.
4. The aim is to accumulate as many points as you can. Keep a record of your score and try to beat it.

TWO OR MORE PLAYERS:

1. Follow the instructions above. For two players, use eight balls each. For three or more players, use six balls each.
2. Players take turns to putt, adding up their points as they go. The game ends when either all the tees have been knocked down or all the players have run out of balls. The highest total score wins. If the score is tied, take one more putt each, aiming at the Ace. The player who finishes closest is the winner.

Want a challenge?

- Try shuffling the cards and placing them in the two rows at random. You could even put them face down and only look at their value once their tee has been knocked over.

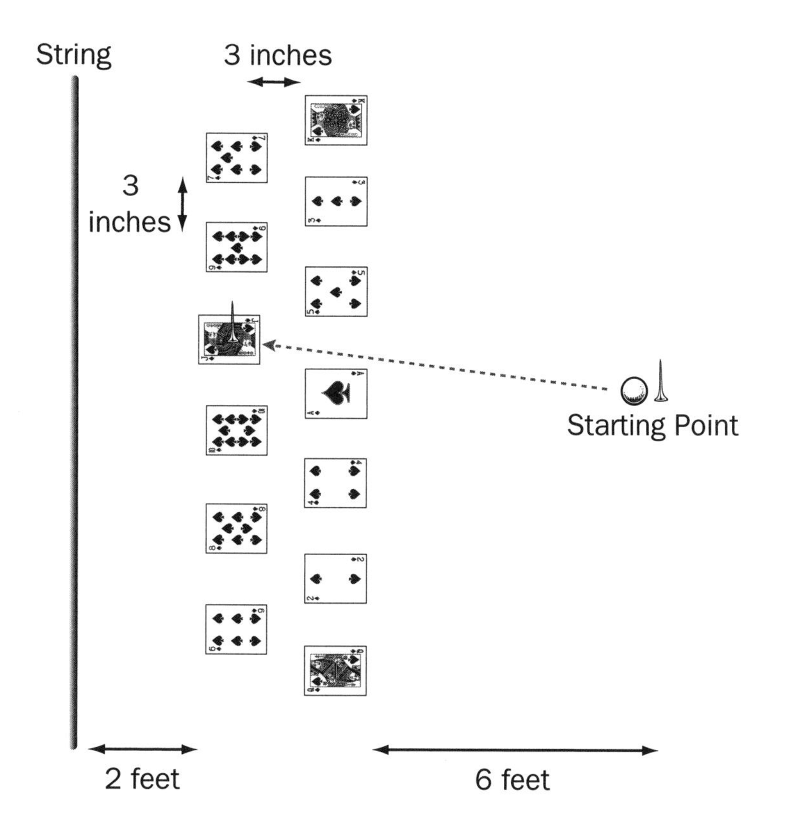

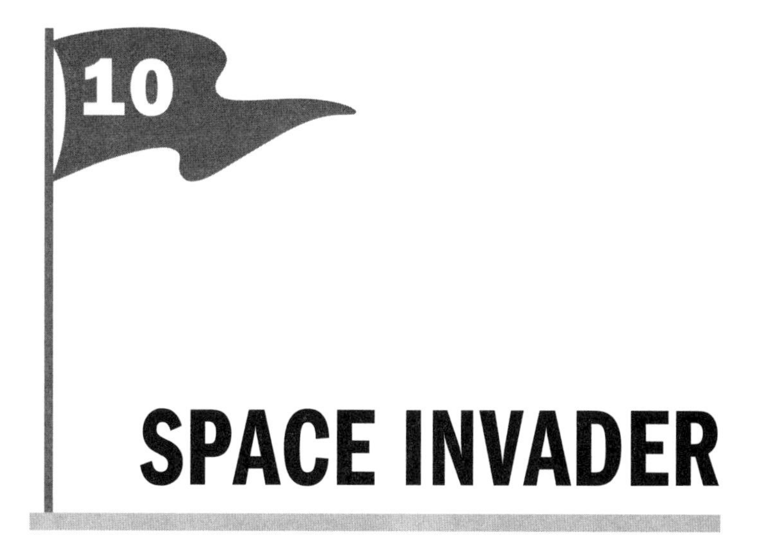

SPACE INVADER

A challenging game of accuracy to help improve the weight of your putts. Can you putt all five balls into the space successfully?

ONE PLAYER:

1. Place four tees to mark the corners of a 3 x 3 foot square, and place a 3-foot length of string between the far tees.
2. Starting about 3 feet away, putt a ball into the square, aiming to make it finish as close to the front as possible.
3. Now putt another ball and try to make it finish between the first ball and the string. The aim of the game is to putt five balls into the square without a ball finishing short of the previous one or crossing the string.
4. If you are successful, start again and try to putt six balls this time. Keep trying to increase the number, and see how many balls you can successfully putt into the square.
5. This game requires that your putts have excellent line as well as length. As the target area gets crowded, you'll need to be accurate with your aim to plot a successful path through the other balls.

TWO OR MORE PLAYERS:

1. Follow the instructions above. The player who successfully putts the most balls into his/her square wins. If it's a tie, take one more putt each. The winner is the player who can get closest to the string without crossing it.

Want a challenge?

- Make the width of the target area narrower.
- Gradually move back and start from farther away.

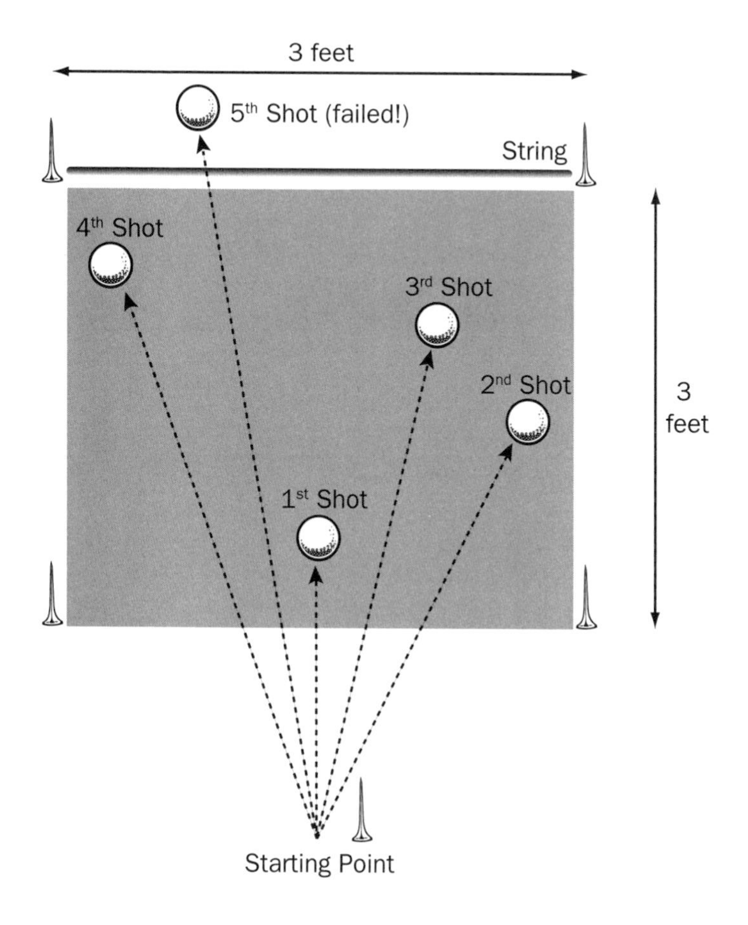

GOLF SOCCER

An exciting game of skill for two players. You'll need solid tactics as well as solid putting if you want to score a goal.

TWO PLAYERS:

1. Use two pairs of tees to set up the goals. Each pair of tees should be 4¼ inches apart (the diameter of a golf hole), and the goals should ideally be about 8 feet away from each other.

2. Each player chooses a side and lines up five balls, 1 foot in front of his/her goal. (If possible, use a different brand or color for each set of balls.)

3. Players take turns putting, playing any one of his/her own balls. The aim is to putt each ball through your opponent's goal.

4. Players have the option to putt their balls into a position that blocks their opponent's shots; however, if they make contact with an opponent's ball, it is a foul and the offender must miss a turn.

5. When a player scores, that ball is removed from the game and the player takes another turn. If a player misses the goal by knocking over a tee or going past the tees without going through them, the ball (and tee) must be returned to its original starting position and the player's turn is over.

6. The winner is the first person to score all five goals.

Want a challenge?

- If a putt misses the goal or knocks over a tee, the ball is not replaced but is removed from the game altogether. In this scenario, the player who scores the most goals is the winner.

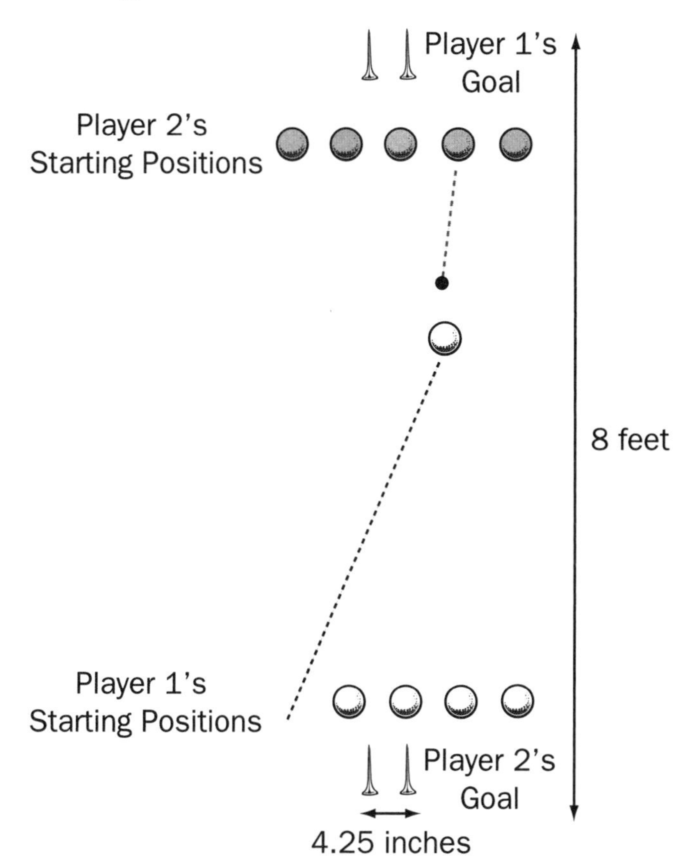

TUNNEL VISION

A simple game designed to sharpen your aim. How far through the tunnel can you putt?

ONE PLAYER:

1. Take fourteen tees and arrange them in two lines (seven tees in each) where each pair of opposite tees gets gradually closer together. The first pair of tees should be 8 inches apart and the last pair 3 inches apart. The tees in each line should be 4 inches apart, forming a tunnel.
2. Place the end tee at the far end of the tunnel. It should be 2 feet from the final pair of tees.
3. Start 3 feet away from the front tees, and try to putt a ball as far as possible through the tunnel without it reaching the end tee. If you knock over any tees (including the end tee), you must start over.
4. The aim is to successfully putt a ball through the tunnel twice in a row. If you achieve this goal, move back 6 inches at a time and try again. How far from the tunnel can you go?

TWO OR MORE PLAYERS:

1. Set up the game as described above, and alternate taking shots from an agreed starting point.
2. Score three points if you successfully putt through the tunnel without knocking over the end tee. If all players fail, the player(s) who made it farthest through the tunnel before knocking over a tee scores one point. The winner is the first player to accumulate ten points.

Want a challenge?

- Increase the distance between the tees in each line to make the tunnel longer.
- To practice the optimum putting speed aim to make each putt finish 17 inches past the tunnel.

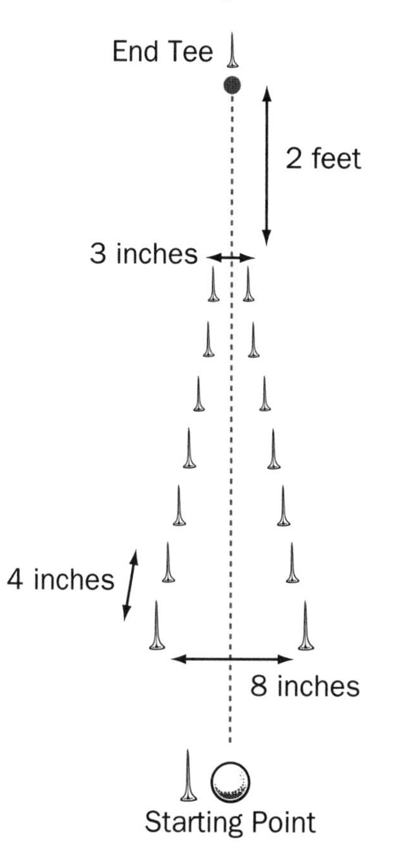

BATTLE ZONE

A strategic game of placement for two players. Will the attacker or the defender prevail?

TWO PLAYERS:

1. For this game you'll need four balls. Player 1 is the *attacker* and uses one ball, and Player 2 is the *defender* and uses two balls. The fourth ball is used as a target ball. (If possible, use a different color or brand for each set of balls.)
2. Player 1 begins by putting the target ball a distance of his/her choice from an agreed starting point.
3. Player 2 then putts two balls and tries to get them as close to the target ball as possible, defending it against Player 1's attack.
4. Player 1 then has one putt to try to get closer to the target ball than either of Player 2's balls.
5. If, after all the balls have been played, Player 1's ball is closest, he/she is awarded two points. If either of Player 2's balls is closest, he/she is awarded one point.
6. Clear the course and start over. Player 1 always chooses the distance of the target ball. The first player to score eight points wins. When the game is over, swap roles and play again. The player with the highest combined score from the two games is the overall winner. If it's a tie, the game moves to sudden death, where each player has one putt to get as close as possible to the target ball. The player with the closest ball is the winner.

Want a challenge?

- Give the defender three balls. The attacker is now awarded three points if he/she is able to putt closest to the target ball.
- For a variation, allow the attacker to choose at what point in the round he/she wants to putt so that the same player doesn't always putt last.

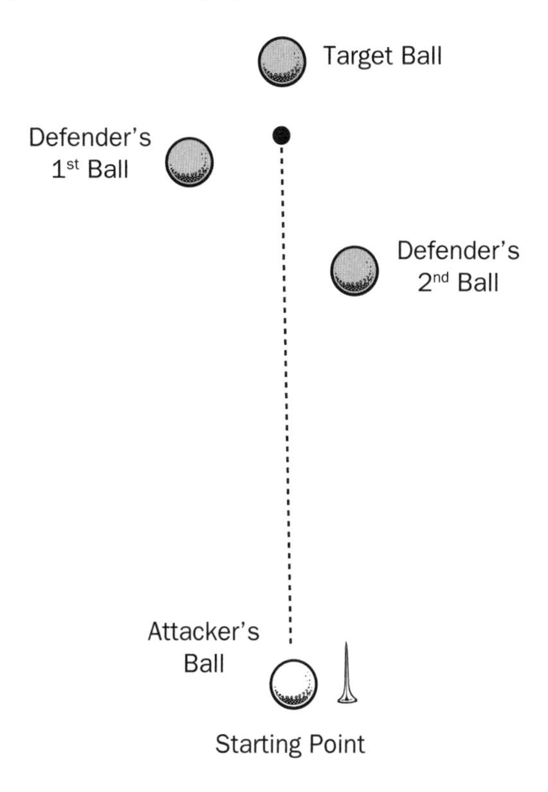

GOLF CROQUET

Design your own course, and try to navigate around it in as few putts as possible.

ONE PLAYER:

1. Place five pairs of tees 4¼ inches apart at various positions around the room. Each pair represents a golf hole. Place an additional tee in the center of the room to serve as the finish tee.
2. Choose a starting point, and plot a route passing through each hole once in as few shots as possible. Putts can pass through the tees in either direction. If you knock over a tee (excluding the finish tee), continue to the next hole but add two penalty strokes to your score.
3. To end the game, you must knock over the finish tee. Vary your starting point and try to beat your score.

TWO OR MORE PLAYERS:

1. Design a course as described above. All players should choose their own starting position and take turns to putt their own way around the course at the same time. They must pass through each hole once in either direction.
2. If a player knocks over a tee, it is replaced in its original position, and the player must start again from the beginning. If you are able to hit an opponent's ball, reward yourself with an extra turn.

3. The first player to pass through each hole and knock over the finish tee is the winner.

Want a challenge?

- Give each hole a number, and choose the order randomly by pulling the numbers out of a hat.
- Add more holes or extend the size of the course.

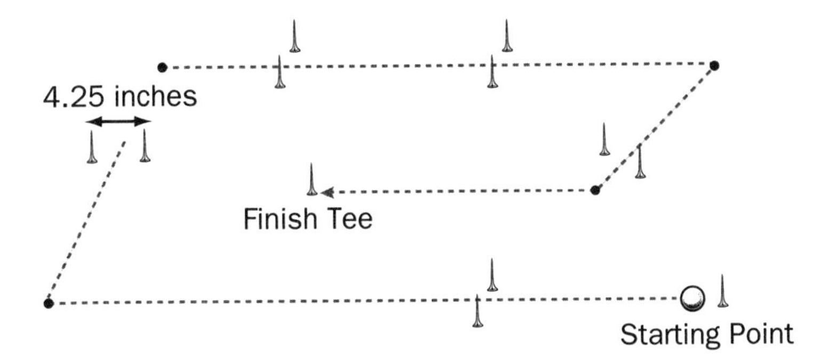

GOLF TENNIS

Speed is the key to this two-player challenge. Who will win the game...set and match?!

TWO PLAYERS:

1. For this game you need fourteen tees. Place two tees in the center of the room, 10 inches apart. The imaginary line between them represents a tennis net.
2. Using the measurements shown, place six more tees on either side of the net to mark out the different scoring zones.
3. Players stand at opposite sides of the net. Player 1 serves first by starting from his/her own Zone 2 and putting the ball across the net into Player 2's court.
4. The serving player earns one, two, or three points, depending on which zone the ball finishes in. If the ball stops between zones, the player is awarded the higher score.
5. Player 2 now takes a turn from wherever the ball came to rest, putting it back into Player 1's court and scoring points accordingly. Both players then rally back and forth, accumulating points. If a ball finishes outside the area of the court or knocks over a tee, no points are awarded for that shot, and the game continues with the other player serving again from his/her own Zone 2.
6. The first person to score twenty points is the winner. Alternatively, you could use real tennis scoring and play games and sets.

Want a challenge?

- Extend the length of Zone 1 or shorten Zone 3.
- *Subtract* points for knocking over tees.

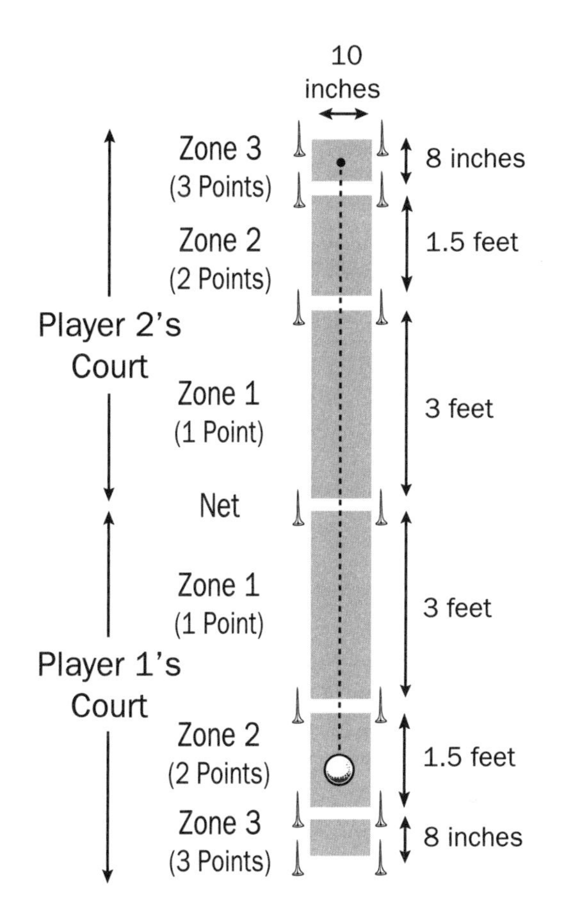

KNOCKOUT

A test of accuracy for two or more players. Knock down all your targets to win the game.

TWO OR MORE PLAYERS:

1. Each player should make a line of five tees at one end of the room. The tees within each line should be 4 inches apart. Place a length of string 2 feet behind the tees.
2. Starting an agreed distance away, Player 1 putts first and aims to knock over one of his/her own set of tees. If successful, Player 1 removes the fallen tee from the playing area and aims to hit another tee. Player 1 continues until he/she misses. It is then Player 2's turn.
3. Putts are not allowed to cross the string. If this happens, the player's turn is also over, and if a tee was knocked down on that putt, it must be replaced.
4. The first person to knock over all of his/her tees is the winner.

Want a challenge?

- Make a rule that the tees must be knocked over in order. To make this even harder, add more tees or place the tees closer together to increase the chances of hitting the wrong one.
- If a ball crosses the string, *all* the tees must be replaced.
- Gradually move back and start from farther away.

- To practice an optimum putting speed, aim to make each putt finish 17 inches past the tees.

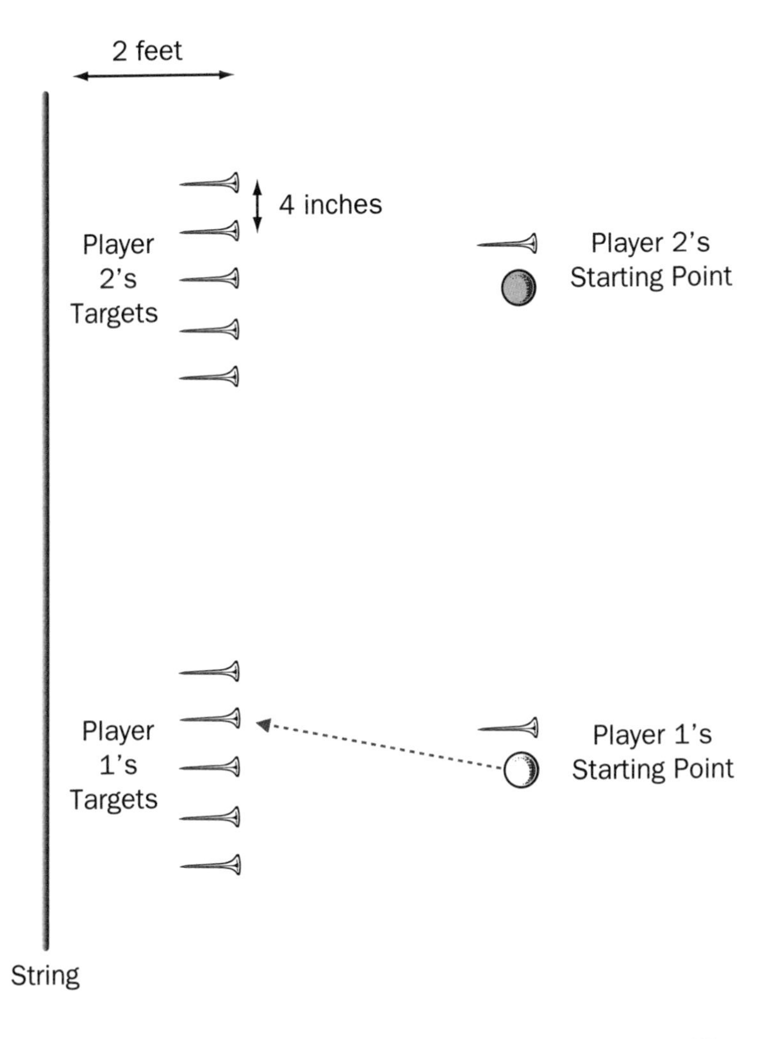

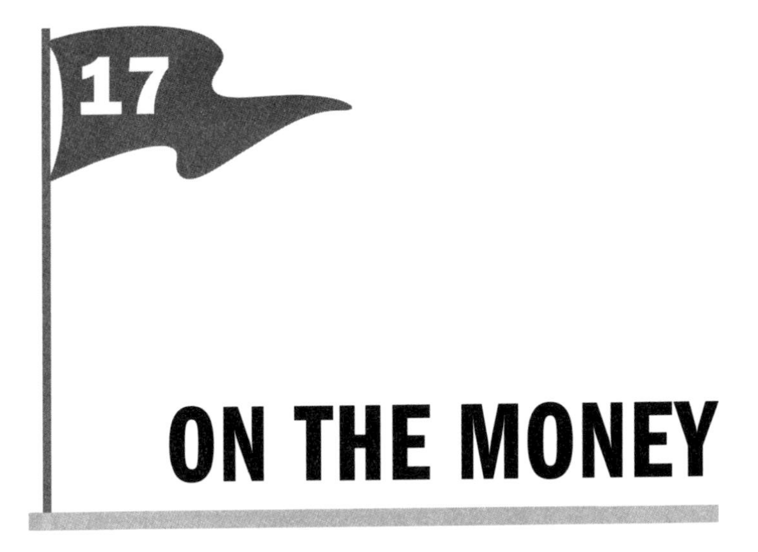

17 ON THE MONEY

An addictive game that proves much harder than it looks. You'll need lots of skill and patience to succeed!

ONE PLAYER:

1. Lay a $1 bill on the floor, and place a tee at a suitable starting point. Eight feet from the bill is a good, challenging length.
2. Try to putt a ball so that it comes to rest on the bill.

TWO OR MORE PLAYERS:

1. Follow the instructions above with each player taking turns putting.
2. The first player to putt a ball that comes to rest on the bill is the winner. If you're feeling generous, the money can be the prize!

Want a challenge?

- If you're able to land the ball on the bill and you really love a challenge, replace the money with a postage stamp. Good luck!

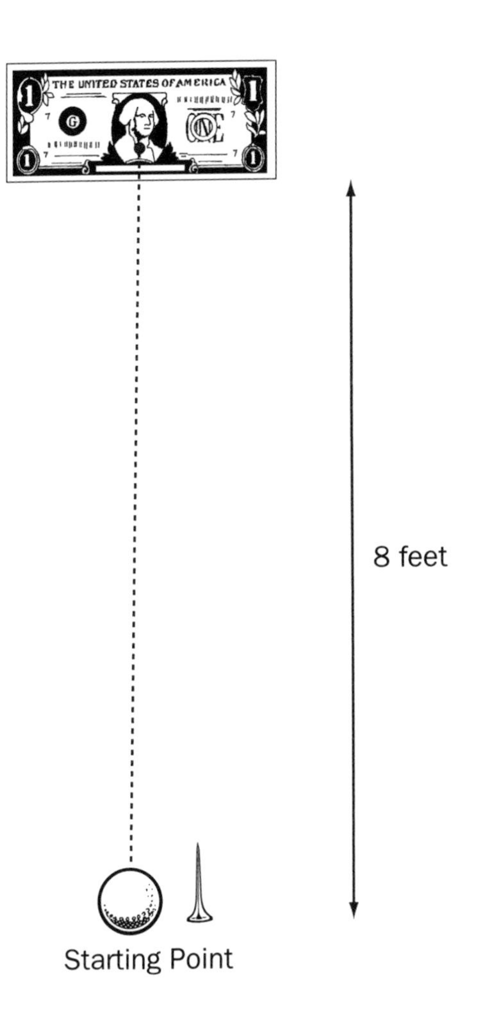
THE UNITED STATES OF AMERICA
8 feet
Starting Point

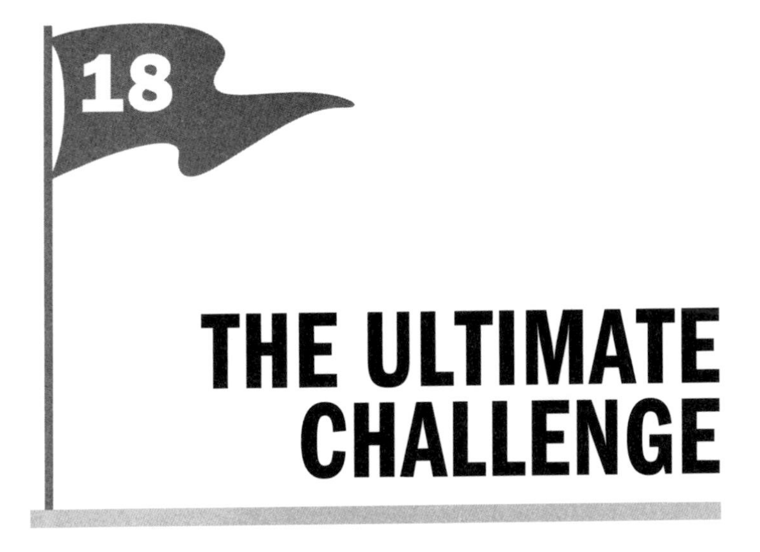

THE ULTIMATE CHALLENGE

The hardest game of all. If you succeed at the Ultimate Challenge, you are an outstanding putter.

ONE PLAYER:

1. Place a cup at the far end of the room, and balance a 12-inch ruler against the rim. (Ideally, the cup should be about 4 inches tall and heavy enough so that it can't be knocked over. If the ball causes the ruler to slide on the cup, affix it with tape.)
2. Starting about 8 feet away, try to putt a ball up the ruler and into the cup. To succeed you must have not only the perfect line but also the perfect pace. If you hit the ball too hard, it will fly over the cup and miss.

TWO OR MORE PLAYERS:

1. Follow the instructions above with each player taking turns putting. The first player to successfully putt a ball into the cup is the winner.

Want a challenge?

- If you are successful, gradually move back and start from farther away. How far from the cup can you stand and still sink the putt?

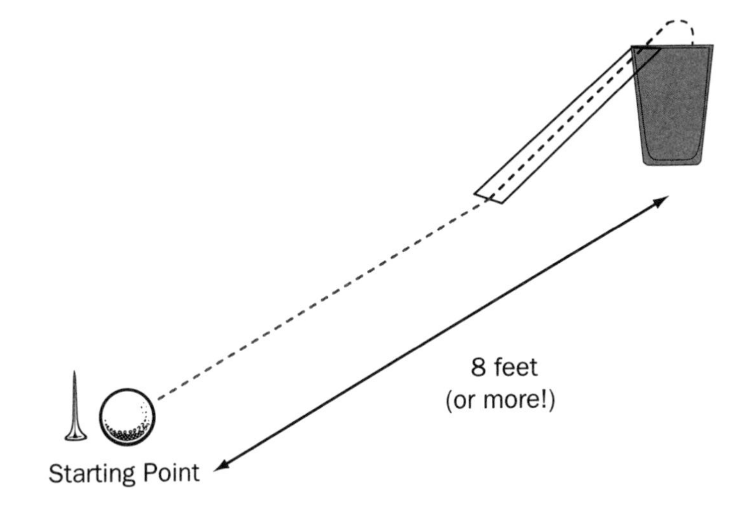
8 feet
(or more!)
Starting Point

THE INDOOR OPEN

Now that you've played all the games, try hosting your own 18-hole tournament. The Indoor Open pits you against your opponents at each game in turn. It's a lot of fun and a great way to practice and improve your putting.

TWO PLAYERS:

1. The tournament begins at Hole 1 with Clock Golf. Follow the game's instructions and see who the winner is.
2. The winner of Hole 1 goes "1 up." (This is a golf term for winning a hole and being one hole in the lead.)
3. Players then move onto Hole 2 (Every Putt Counts) and see who the winner of this game is.
4. If the same player wins both the first two holes, he/she is now "2 up." If the loser of the first hole wins the second hole, the score goes back to "all square" for the tournament. (This means they have both won the same number of holes and are therefore currently tied.)
5. Play each game in turn and keep track of the score. The tournament continues until one player has a lead that can't be caught. When this happens, the tournament ends and the winner is the Indoor Open Champion!

THREE OR MORE PLAYERS:

For a tournament involving more than two players, you have the following options:

- Skip Holes 11, 13, and 14 since these games have been designed for two players only, and play a tournament of 15 holes instead.

OR

- Play Holes 11, 13, and 14 as a round-robin game between all the players. The overall winner wins the hole. This way every game is included and the tournament can be all 18 holes.

In both scenarios, players should keep a record of how many holes they win. The player with the highest total is the Indoor Open Champion!

THE INDOOR OPEN SCORECARD

Use the scorecard on the next page to keep track of who wins each hole and see who the overall champion is.

HOLE	NAME	WINNER'S NAME AND MATCH SCORE
1	Clock Golf	
2	Every Putt Counts	
3	Slalom Golf	
4	The Five-Box Challenge	
5	Ten-Pin Golf	
6	Last Ball Standing	
7	Minefield	
8	Distance Challenge	
9	Target Practice	
10	Space Invader	
11	Golf Soccer	
12	Tunnel Vision	
13	Battle Zone	
14	Golf Tennis	
15	Golf Croquet	
16	Knockout	
17	On the Money	
18	The Ultimate Challenge	
	The Indoor Open Champion	

ABOUT THE AUTHOR

Adrian Winter has been playing golf for nearly 30 years, winning a number of tournaments and putting championships. Originally from Surrey, England, he has played golf on 5 continents and coached both in the UK and abroad. He is currently based in China where he teaches at a university near Hong Kong.